AF200469

Business Plan Handbook

Practical guide to create a business plan

Dipl.-Kfm. (FH) Arthur Lämmle

Am Tannenberg 4

97877 Wertheim

Bibliographic information of the German national library:

The German national library registers this publication in the German national bibliography; specified bibliographic data are retrievable on the Internet at dnb.dnb.de.

© 2020 Dipl.-Kfm. (FH) Arthur Lämmle

Manufactured and published by

BoD – Books on Demand, Norderstedt

ISBN: 9 – 78 37 51 – 91 42 60

Table of contents...................................... I-III

I

II

III

1. Introduction

The creation of a business concept (business plan) for a business idea is not only reserved for large companies or corporate consultations but also for small enterprises and private individuals. In addition, the elaboration of such a business concept is not bound to any industry.

This results in countless application possibilities for business concepts and just as broadly as the different possibilities are, is the scope laid down in the elaboration.

The overall plan includes a complete view of input, output, performance, profitability, liquidity, legal and tax-related aspects, as well as an assessment of the potential, the business opportunities, and risks over a long period of time.[1]

A business plan applies not only to internal but also to external stakeholder groups as a complete and plausible concept to check the feasibility of a business idea or project.

---

[1] Kubicek, Herbert; Brückner, Steffen (2009): p. 1

If business concepts (business plans) are feasible, then they are also being used as standard instruments to attract lenders, employees, customers, long-term business partners, or successors.

In practice, there are countless books that can be used in the editing process, but only a few manuals which provide a clear overview of the topics and are able to guide you through the process.

But when it comes to successfully implementing a project with the immense use of time, resources, and human workforce, it is important to have a manual that briefly presents the necessary requirements and also describes important recommendations for action.

The following document is a business plan handbook which not only guides the reader step by step through the process in order to create a holistic business concept but also taking professional standards into account.

Professional standards are understood as scientifically recognized methods, or are based on dominant approaches in practice, or orientate themself on the legislator's guidelines. Therefor one will asure an objective and a realistic approach.

At the beginning **general requirements** or so-called **principles** which are essential for a business plan are clarified in order to deal with the actual requirements of a business plan in the main part. The business plan can be divided into three areas.

The **first part** describes the company and consists of the following chapters: company presentation, factory and operating equipment, management and organization, market and competitors.

In the **second part** the right strategies are developed by using a marketing concept and a SWOT-Analysis.

In the **third part** an economic approach takes place. The so-called financial plan consist of a opening balance sheet, profit and loss account, as well as liquidity planning.

In the end all relevant information and facts are presented in an **Executive Summary**.

The requirements for a business plan are described using the following central questions which are addressed in each chapter as required:

- ✓ What needs to be done?

- ✓ Why does it have to be done?

- ✓ How is it done?

- ✓ What is the result?

- ✓ Where is the result taken into account in the business plan or financial plan?

- ✓ What further literature can be used?

2. General requirements[2]

General requirements are not tied to the content but rather define principles that a business plan has to fulfill in order to be a professional and meaningful business concept. In the following are nine general requirements briefly described.

At the **external appearance** a great deal of care and accuracy is given. In order to preserve the external form one should not only think about spelling mistakes, font, and size, but also about the title page, a detailed structure, and how it should ultimately be bound. The viewer or reader quickly gets such details and these details have a positive or negative impact on the assessment of the concept as well as the performance of the founding team.

In order for a business plan to be understandable to everyone it is important to ensure that the context is presented in a **comprehensible manner**. Note that, a clear structure and short sentences makes it easier to read. In addition, the entire business plan must not be too long. A range from about 30 to 40 pages is standard. This ensures the attention of the reader to the last sentence.

---

[2] Klandt, Heinz ; Finke-Schürmann, Tanja (2000): p. 57 - 63

The **completeness** of a business plan is not easy to achieve. It is therefore recommended to complete the business plan as extensively as possible on the basis of literature, experts, or checklists. If there are gaps, make sure that they are also being described. Appropriate sub planning or partial aspects shall be attached to the appendix.

In order to convey **credibility** it is necessary to argue objectively, to name weaknesses, and risks. The information or data generated through the process should be well-founded and verifiable. Once again, identified gaps need be addressed in order to ensure greater transparency and promote trust.

Flexibility means adaptability to changing initial conditions. Even, if one assumes that all the information which the calculations and forecasts are based on are correct, it can nevertheless happen that the initial conditions such as buyer behavior or competitive structure develop differently. That is why it is extremely important that the company concept and the assumptions are constantly questioned.

A business concept always orientates itself on the **targeted group**. It means, that one creates a business plan with the goal to convince a specific group of a business idea. If someone want to convince, for example, a stratigic partner, then topics like common cooperation or common service creation are brought to the fore. Or someone want to win new investors or lenders, then the focus switches to the financial planning. On the other hand, if someone is trying to reach potential customers, then the right arguments are found in the chapter „marketing concept". At any case, one will ensure an appropriate argumentation by presenting the relevant information from the targeted group´s point of view.

A business concept not only relays on high quality **information and data** but also on estimations and forecasts. Therefore, it is recommended to point out, how specific values are put together. If one has laid down reliable information and data, then the credibility and the chance of realization rises.

The **Timeframe** is another important aspect in the editing process of a business plan. Normally, a planning horizon between three and five years is appropriate. Periods between ten and fifteen years are conceivable if the business plan does require it. In a large timeframe it is checked whether the business concept can be realized in a fixed timeframe and also has the possibility to exist at the market long term.

The last general requirement on a business concept refers to the **financial planning**. It is important to include a revenue plan and a liquidity plan. The revenue plan shows whether the company´s earnings are positive or negative. The liquidity plan on the other hand gives information whether one can handle payment obligations on schedule. A precis view at the deposits and payments gives one the opportunity to anticipate payment bottlenecks that can lead to bankruptcy and failure.

Requirements on a company presentation

Step 1: As a first step, the initial situation is described in detail and aptly. It mentions authors, founders, and involved parties. In this context it is also important to describe why the business idea was developed. Instructions for an elaboration can be found in chapter 3.1 „starting point".

Step 2: The second step describes the actual business idea (chapter 3.2). These includes the product, service, as well as the customer benefits. The presentation of the business idea can also be facilitated by embedding it into a value chain, or by describing relevant strategic partners and market participants.

Step 3: Description and presentation of a company´s vision that moves between three and five years. In addition, all important company´s milestones necessary to achieve the vision are recorded. The exact procedure can be found in chapter 3.3 „company´s vision and missions".

3. Company presentation

Basically, the presentation of the company consists of the description of the starting situation, business idea, and company´s vision.[3] The Goal is to indicate that it is possible to transfer the competences and experiences of the past into the future.[4]

If necessary, the company presentation can also be extended by two chapters. On the one hand, the business idea can be arranged in a customary value-added chain, or on the other hand describe important and relevant business partners. Thereby the commercial or business idea can be described more easily.

3.1 Starting point

The description of the starting point can concern two initial scenarios. Either an already existing company which would like to expand provides an entire and plausible business concept or a new establishment occurs through a private person, a company, or community.

---

[3] Klandt, Heinz ; Finke-Schürmann, Tanja (2000): p. 71
[4] Nagl, Anna (2006): p. 21

Many new establishments fail not because of the lack of a good business idea but the ability to realize the business concept.[5] Therefore, it is important to describe, who is the originator of the business idea, since when does the business idea exists, and whether comparable products or services are already offered by the market.[6]

If a connection between originators and business idea is evident, then a basic consensus as well as a very strong intrinsic motivation can be assumed, which combines the participating people and organization. At the end, by finish reading this chapter it is already possible to identify how long or intensely someone grappled with a business idea.[7]

As soon as a new enterprise is founded from a private person the essential aspects of the description vary in some regard. Instead of the description of the company a detailed description of the founder's team moves into focus. Note, the qualifications of the founder's team play a secondary role in this chapter.

[5] Wodon, Christian; Gründerservice der Wirtschaftskammer Wien (2012): p. 27 - 28
[6] Klandt, Heinz ; Finke-Schürmann, Tanja (2000): p. 71
[7] Klandt, Heinz ; Finke-Schürmann, Tanja (2000): p. 23

The relevant questions at this point are: How did the business idea come into existence? Who are or were the involved people?[8]

The following example will illustrate the process.

The founder Alan Anderson has a university degree in the field Bachelor of Science and was engaged with his colleague, Matthias Lothar, on high performance construction boards. The idea came Alan Anderson during a project to increase the clocking performance of resistors. During his analysis he found out, that not only the resistor itself but also the construction board is significantly involved in raising the output capacity. Both founders are supported by the chair of business informatics and system development of the university Stuttgart. The main supporter in particular was professor Dr. Alvin Klein who helped to convert the idea into success. To transform this research project into a potential spin-off, the following business concept was developed.

[8] Kubicek, Herbert ; Brückner, Steffen (2009): p. 72

If the initial situation is described in detail, then the description of the business idea itself follows as the second step.

3.2 Buiness idea

3.2.1 Product and service policy

To describe a business idea appropriately, it requires in most cases no more than three sentences to generate the necessary attention. If one has gained the attention, it is time to persuade the business partners of the benefits.

Concerning the content, three questions have to be answered at this point: What will be produced? For whom will it be produced? What uses or benefits are generated?[9]

At this stage of the business plan one describes the products and the services in detail. During the elaboration one will get a feeling for the service creation, production process, need-satisfaction, as well as for the core of the enterprise.

---

[9] Klandt, Heinz ; Finke-Schürmann, Tanja (2000): p. 71

In the early stage one limit himself commonly to three to five products or services to reduce the planing effort as well as the complexity.[10]

Product or service	Core product or service	Who ist he main client?	What ist he benefit?
Electric construc-tion board	5 x 10 cm	Manufacturer of network controller, graphic cards, mainboards, and laptops in Germany.	Commercial use of twelve core processors without additional power consumption.
	10 x 15 cm		
	15 x 15 cm		
	15 x 20 cm		
	20 x 20 cm		

Table No. 1: Determination of the core products or services

The chapters 3.2.1 „key products and services", 3.2.2 "customer value", and 6.3 "customer analysis" can support one by formulating the commercial idea. Appropriate literature from the area of Marketing, especially product and service policies, can be used as advanced material to gain additional information.

---

[10] Wodon, Christian; Gründerservice der Wirtschaftskammer Wien (2012): p. 23

3.2.2 Customer value

If one has described the products or the services and has defined the customers or target groups, then it is time to identify the uses and benefits.

The description of the customer uses and benefits is important because the use consists of four dimensions and not every use, benefit, or advantage is immediately evident for the customer.

If the use or benefit is identified, one can refer to them accordingly to persuade the customers or business associates.

The customer use or benefit consists of quality, price, time factor, and service.[11]

The following example will illustrate the process.

---

[11] Camphausen, Bernd (2008): p. 159 - 160

Quality: Through our special construction method and under the use of special electrical resistors the construction boards dispose the same energy consumption while producing higher tact frequency than the branded goods which are available at the moment.

Price: With an adequate delivery quantity and long-term supply agreement prices can be realized which orientate themselves at the market price or even less.

Time factor: Despite of our short delivery times reorders are usually available within two weeks.

Service: In addition, our service offers the possibility to take care of individual customer wishes without creating additional costs.

The advantages for the customers arise not only from the product or service directly but also what is typically available at the market. From chapters 6.1 "market analysis", 6.2 "competitive analysis", and 6.3 "customer analysis" additional advantages can be identified.

3.3 Company´s vision and missions

The company´s vision describes the state of the enterprise in a period between three and five years. To achieve the company´s vision or target state, single missions are set up which are necessary to realize the vision.[12]

There are a number of different reasons to become self-employed. For example, one can fulfill himself or build up a livelihood. However, one can also combine both. Other reasons to start a new commercial activity can be, for example, expansion, and growth objectives.

If one has found out what the reason for the given plan is, then one takes notes where the trip goes, or how it should look, or where one would like to be in five years.

As a result, one will receive a number of missions or landmarks which must be achieved in order to let the company´s vision shape up in reality.

---

[12] Wodon, Christian; Gründerservice der Wirtschaftskammer Wien (2012): p. 34

For a business plan it is necessary to set up three to five missions or landmarks. Nevertheless, these goals must be specific, measurable, achievable, relevant, and time-bound.

The knowledge, which is gained through the process, is indispensable for the further planning. Since one knows where the trip goes, then one can also plan a way there. The following example will illustrate the process.

The founder's team consists of Mathias Lothar and Alan Anderson. They have set up a vision to become one of the top five manufacturers of construction boards in Europe. The company´s name as well as the products should be associated with quality, longevity, and excellent service. In order to achieve this vision small steps or single missions must be fulfilled. After the missions are set up it is necessary to sort them by time sequence. The time sequence of missions tells one which goals have to be achieved in order to let the vision shape up in reality. One calls such list of missions „**landmarks of the company**".[13]

---

[13] Karbach, Rolf ; Niederle, Jan (2004): p. 20ff

In one year:

First industrially produced construction board. Supplier's contracts with top five manufacturers of network cards, laptops, and servers in Germany.

In two years:

Turnover of 300,000.- € and a profit of at least 120,000.- €. Additional recruitment of staff at the sales department and administration.

In three years:

Analysis of the market and the competitors in France, Switzerland, and Austria. Clarification of juridically as well as technical questions concerning application and use restrictions of the product or service in the well-chosen countries.

In three and a half years:

Sales planning, branch planning, as well as analysis of the customer´s preferences in the well-chosen countries for the adjustment of product, price, communication, and distribution policies.

Requirements on factory and operating equipment

Step 4: At this step, one describes in detail what is necessary to start the business activity or service. Into consideration has to be taken business equipment, operating materials, and employees.

Step 5: To start the business activity and be successful in doing so the enterprise has to dispose suitable employees or staffs. So, at this step, one describes which core competence are of essential importance for the start up or enterprise.

Step 6: As a final step to check the requirements of the chapter factory and operating material, one will describe all legal requirements which have to be respected to start the business activities successfully. An evaluation of optional seals or labels can be taken into consideration.

4. Factory and operating equipment

In this chapter, it is necessary to analyze everything what is needed to start the business activity successfully. Thereby, one allows himself to generate an overview of the investments that has to be made. And therefor, one can also determine the capital requirements and the running costs.

The implementation refers to business equipment and production, as for example, business premises, office equipment, operating material, and necessary workforce. If important practical skills are required by the workforce or only a limited number of suppliers is available at the market, then it is recommended to describe it in detail and professional.

In addition, a location analysis can be generated at this point, as well as an arrangement and presentation of an in-house quality assurance.

Besides, one has to approve, for example, trademark protection, patent rights, or technical requirements in order to fulfill the feasibility of a project. At the end, one receives sub plans, as for example, investment plans, write-off plans, cost plans, production and procurement plans, or whole job profiles.[14]

4.1 Production factors

4.1.1 Business premises

In this segment, one takes note on all necessary business premises. It includes the planned size as well as all additional costs. So, one can analyze the total and exact costs in the second step. As a result, one receives an overview of the single facilities with their specific size which are already available or have to be procured. On the other side, one will receive data in the form of the costs which are considered in the budgetary planning.

To be exact, one approaches the subject by taking note of the size for necessary facilities, as for example, distribution, management, manufacturing, and possibly storage. Then, one enquires through trade offices or real estate agents what the market prices are, so that a calculation close to reality can be fulfilled.

---

[14] Kubicek, Herbert ; Brückner, Steffen (2009): p. 91

Besides, it is also common to calculate, for example, the servicing and maintenance work, energy and water consumption, waste disposal, or special security measures. Expenses like these can be found under the topic additional costs. At the end one will receive such an exemplary representation.[15]

Business Premises	Square meter	€ per sqare meter	€ per month
Administrative office	25	11	275,-
Production hall	250	18	4.500,-
Workshop	150	8	1.200,-
Storage	500	7	3.500,-
Retail store	45	35	1.575,-
Research and Development	300	12	3.600,-
Sales offices	35	14	490,-
Additional costs			3.000,-
In total	**1305**		**18.140,-**

Table No.: 2: Running costs of business premises

---

[15] Klandt, Heinz ; Finke-Schürmann, Tanja (2000): p. 120 - 128

4.1.2 Factory equipment

In this chapter, one puts together everything what is necessary to assure a smooth workflow for the departments like procurement, production, management, administration, distribution, as well as research and development. This includes technical devices, machines, the whole office equipment, for example, computers, pencils, chairs, and desks.

By generating such an overview it reveals itself fast what is still required and what already exists. Moreover, a cost analysis which is considered in the budgetary planning can be managed properly in this way.[16]

From the overview of the factory equipment list one can identify the capital assets of the enterprise. The fixed assets of the enterprise are subject to decline of value.

Therefore, according to the selected write-off method the production or acquisition costs have to be proportionately spread over the whole duration of use.

---

[16] Klandt, Heinz ; Finke-Schürmann, Tanja (2000), p. 125 - 126

For further information the chapter 9.4.2 "investment and depreciation planning" is recommended.

Factory equipment	Existing in €	Acquire in €
2 x Business cars		30.000,-
5 x Shelving units		3.500,-
Forklift truck		25.000,-
2 x Pallet trucks		2.500,-
Laboratory equipment		1.800,-
5 x Desktops		1.350,-
3 x Personal computers		2.180,-
Laser machine		45.000,-
...		
Total costs:		111.330,-

Table No.: 3: Exemplary representation of a business equipment list

4.1.3 Operating equipment

If one will finde himself in the production or service industry, then materials and goods are to be procured prematurely to assure production or service without friction. Therefore, it is to be outlined in advanced on how the procurement modalities of the company will look like.

Besides, by describing materials and goods, it is important to explain whether the materials are standardized, high-quality, or unique pieces. Moreover, is to be stated, who are the suppliers and how long does the delivery take.[17]

If one is bound to sub products or semi-finished products, then one depends on the quality and reliability of the suppliers. Are already provisional agreements with potential suppliers in existence, so one should mention them at this point.

Operating equipment	Existing in €	Aquiring in €	Supplier	Shipping time
Print paper				
Oil and lubricants				
Envelops				
Subproduct				
Raw material X				
Labels				
…..				
Total costs:				

Table No.: 4: Exemplary list of necessary operating materials and equipment

As soon as bigger projects or orders accrue, then it is common that materials, services, or other expenses have to be financed. The reason is that in many cases the payment of the customer mostly becomes due by delivery. So, in the sales process several weeks can pass from the financing up

[17] Klandt, Heinz ; Finke-Schürmann, Tanja (2000): p. 126 – 127

to the payment of the customer. In these cases, it is important that the most likely occurring expenses, for which one must step in, are calculated and listed in advance. Therefore, one avoids financial bottlenecks which can lead to insolvency.

A detailed list of the probable occurring costs or expenses can help to avoid this kind of inconveniences. The following approach will illustrate the process.

Profect / Contract	Which kind of costs will result in advanced payments?	Occurring costs in €
Subproduct 1	Electricity and rent	
	Goods and materials	
	Personnel costs	
	Delivery costs	
	Interest rates	
Subproduct 2	Electricity and rent	
	Goods and materials	
	Personnel costs	
	Deliver costs	
Total costs:		

Table No.: 5: Exemplary calculation of financing big orders in advance

In addition, it is also necessary to take factory and business equipment costs into consideration. Now, the as precise as possible calculated costs are being transferred into in the budgetary planning. Be aware, that the costs occurre in the budgetary planning at the exact payment date and as accurately as possible.

4.1.4 Core competences

Enterprises in the foundation phase depend very strongly on the qualities of the founders. The right people at the right position make the difference, because only then an above-average performance appears.

At this point, it is necessary not only to list important core competences but also advanced information or requirements that go hand in hand. For example, the yearly salary, legal demands, health, safety, or special training courses.[18]

To meet the requirements in this chapter one can orientate himself by the usual functional divisions, for example, production, sales, or distribution.

For instance, a technological enterprise has usually to assure a high quality in research and development as well as marketing. Therefore, one describes the technical, profes-

---

[18] Klandt, Heinz ; Finke-Schürmann, Tanja (2000), p. 127 - 128

sional, social, operational competences that have to be met by the personnel at a certain functional division.

At the end of a detailed description of essential qualifications and competences job profiles are created. This job profiles represent the core competences that the enterprise needs to acquire or develop in order to be successful.

The following example will illustrate the process.

Functional area	Qualifications/ Competences
Research and Development	Concluded study as a Bachelor of Science
	Experiences in project management
	5-year work experience as a mechatronic technician
	Team ability, analytic perceptive facility, and aim-oriented deployment of labor
	Knowledge of the newest developing software for transistors
Sales	Communication ability, contract creation, legal, and technical knowledge
Production	Knowledge in dealing with laser machines, CNC, industrial safety, environment protection, and quality management
Distribution	Packaging and dispatch, stacker's light, loading and cargo protection, create cargo papers under observance of international terms of delivery and dispatch terms

Table No. 6: Identification of core competences

If a subsidiary or a branch office of an already existing enterprise was founded, then the business plan expands accordingly. In this case, for example, not only a detailed description of the core competence but also a description of the organization is requested.

Should one plan with a larger workforce, then it is necessary to name the responsible executives, the allocation of responsibilities, and managerial authorities. If so, one will be able to present the structure of the organization in an organizational chart. A detailed illustration, how it has to be done, can be found in chapter 5 „management and organization".

4.2 Legal requirements[19]

Other challenges with the realization of a business idea are affected by legal demands like laws, policies, and regulations. Main parts of the considerations consist of the business activity themselves, the product, the storage, transport, waste disposal, production, and location.

The decision by which legal regulations an enterprise is affected often requires special knowledge. Regarding this

---

[19] Kubicek, Herbert ; Brückner, Steffen (2009): p. 98 - 99

special knowledge, information can be gathered at the Chamber of Commerce and Industry, environmental agencies, and innovational consulting companies, as well as trade offices.

The obtaining of necessary legal regulations, gathering licenses and approvals have two effects. On the one hand, due to the proceedings, the admission of the commercial activity can be delayed and on the other hand the procedures are generating costs which have to be take into account. Especially at the profit and loss calculation as well as at the liquidity planning.

After all, from project to project one will be unable to avoid voluntary certifications or recognized seals. Voluntary certificates and recognized seals, on the contrary to the legal regulations, can be used for marketing and advertising purposes.

Certificates and seals are mostly based on product or performance criteria. For example, the "TCO seal" or the "CO_2-Footprint" are voluntary certificates that are not necessary but a good advantage if one will display how environmentally friendly the products or services are.

Requirements regarding structures and procedures referring to the enterprise itself are to be found for quality and environmental management in the normalized line „EN ISO 9000 and 14000".

Measures like certificates and seals can be used to show that the company is working within professional standards as well as to increase the company´s reputation and image.

Such measures are valued very high during a market entry, because thus will help to advertise the products, services, and trust within the involved interest group. The following exemplary array will illustrate the process.

The costs which emerge during the realization of the legal measures are being adopted in the budgetary planning under the topic "factory equipment".

In which areas are legal demands welcome or unavoidable?	How are legal demands guaranteed?	Costs of legal require-ments in €	Duration of imple-mentation
Environmental protection	Conversion of DIN EN ISO 14001 by an environmental representative	5,500 € per month	8 to 12 weeks
Health and Safty	Application of DIN EN ISO 45001, company arrangement, expert and company doctor		
Quality management	Integration of DIN EN ISO 9000 and permanent training of the employees		
Accountancy	Observance of the code of commercial law and tax right		
Total expenses and whole duration to achieve legal requirements:			

Table No. 7: Exemplary list of legal requirements, considering information of costs and the duration of implementation

Requirements on management and organization

Step 7: Describe the founder's team, management, as well as the required staff which is available or needed for the enterprise to be successful. In chapter 4.1.4 "core competences" skills and experiences were already identified which now are being assigned to certain employees.

Step 8: Presentation of an organizational structure (organization chart) of the company, concerning the management and communication structure but also the structure of responsibilities.

Step 9: Within this step, one will decide which legal form is more suitable. First, one determines all relevant criteria for the choice of the legal form and then puts the available legal forms in contrast.

5. Management and organization[20]

Successful enterprises are dependent not only on an innovative idea but also on the involved people. Especially professional investors place a lot of value on if it comes to personnel.

Besides, the description of the management or founder's team a business plan also encloses information, regarding the organizational construction as well as the selected legal form.

As a result, one will receive part plans, for example, personnel planning or an organizational chart which includes the structure of responsibilities.

5.1 Management or founding team

At this point, one describes the management or founder's team which is available or needed for the realization.

A big part of the description of abilities and skills are, for example, qualifications, work experiences, or promising industrial expertise. Importantly, one has to identifie as many

---

[20] Kubicek, Herbert ; Brückner, Steffen (2009): p. 172

as possible core competences which are being covert by the founder's team. If certain competences are not available, it is necessary to describe the discrepancy at this point as well as which external sources are being used to compensate the missing competences.

Among useful external resources one will find auditors, lawyers, advertising agencies, management consultants, or tax advisers.

For a detailed coverage of the personnel planning during the foundation phase the chapter „Einstellen von Personal" from the book "Existenzgründung" written by Prof. Dr. Andreas Wien is recommended.

The following table will illustrate the process of describing the qualifications and competence of the management or founder's team.

Name	Qualifications and Competences
Mathias Lothar	Three years of work experience as a distribution employee in the building industry
	Project cooperation in the area of financing and expansion of strategical business segments in the glass industry
	Construction of commercial and sales structures for an IT service provider
Andreas Anderson	Business management study at the university of Würzburg with main focus on marketing and finances
	Project cooperation in the product and market management for an industrial enterprise
	Project cooperation in the planning, implementation, and control of an exhibition for hydraulic pumps
unallocated	Server and data bank administration
	Web technology and e-business

Table No. 8: Exemplary description of the management or founding team

5.2 Organizational structure and process

The success of an enterprise is determined not only by the product but also on basis of the work routines and their structures.

In this chapter, it has to be decided first, when, where, what, and how the duties are fulfilled, and secondly, who will accomplish those duties. The aim is to provide an efficient utilization of the personnel.[21]

To approach an efficient solution one will consider first, which duties are necessary to accomplish in order to reach the enterprise's aims. By doing so, one orientates himself by the traditional functional areas as procurement, production, sales, and distribution.

Then, for every functional area it will be checked, which duties are necessary to the entire fulfilment. The subdivisions can be divided by responsibilities, products, or customer groups.

It depends on, which kind of specialization is relevant in order to guarantee a successful accomplishment of tasks. At the end this procedure will originate a hierarchical structure of tasks and responsibilities.[22]

---

[21] Nagl, Anna (2006): p. 61
[22] Kubicek, Herbert ; Brückner, Steffen (2009): p. 184 – 185

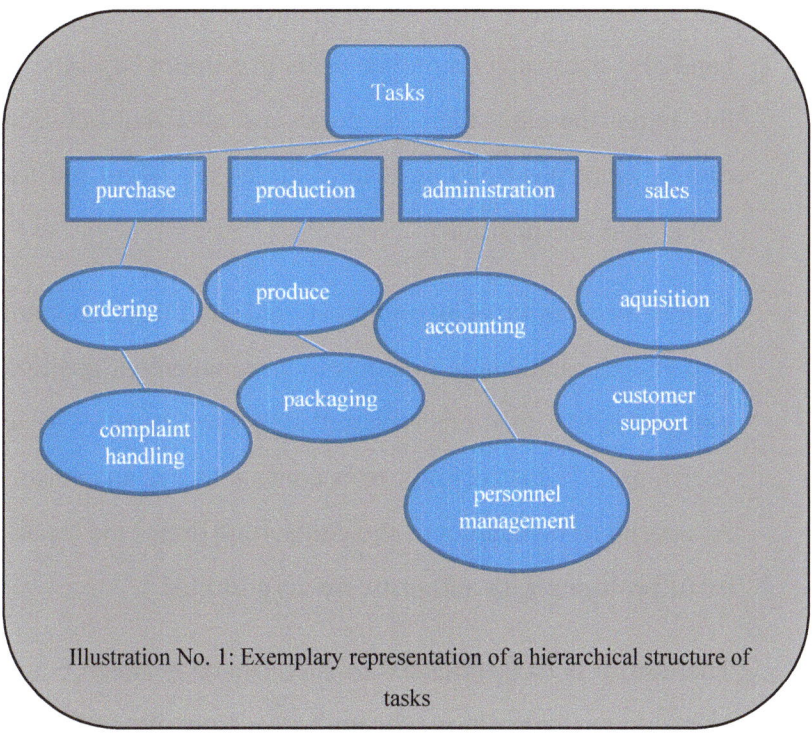

Illustration No. 1: Exemplary representation of a hierarchical structure of tasks

Therefor, in the second step, one will develop on the basis of the structure of tasks an organizational chart, so that an exact allocation of authorizations and responsibilites can be aligned. Now, the organizational chart can simultaneously be used for each interest group as an understandable and plausible guide.

A position is laid out on the capacity of a person´s totality of duties. It has to be checked whether the range of tasks can be mastered by a person permanently and on the other hand also uses each employee to its maximum capacity. If this is not the case, then the duties are allocated between two or more positions or several duties are being put together into one position.

During the creation of an organizational chart it is important to mandate each single position to a management position with authority. Positions with authority have to make basic decisions, give instructions, or become active as an advisor. As a result of management and controlling duties the capacity of positions with authority are very limited.

Therefor, it is recommended to subordinate between 6 and 12 positions to a position with authority. Regarding this topic, it is also common to create intermediaries. For example: Group leader X, project managers Y, or sales manager for region Z.[23]

The following exemplary representation will help to illustrate the process.

[23] Kubicek, Herbert ; Brückner, Steffen (2009): p. 185 - 186

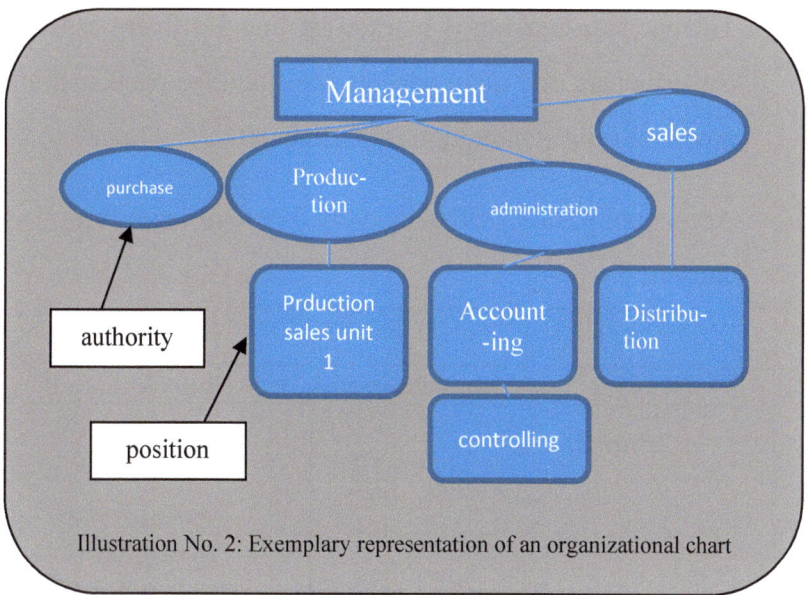

Illustration No. 2: Exemplary representation of an organizational chart

5.3 Legal form

The choice of the legal form for a company is not only for-mality but also decides in the long term on the internal and external relationships between the enterprise and the foun-der.

On the one hand the legal form governs the intern and external relations between the founders and the company, on the other hand the legal form has also concrete tax and economic effects.

The decision-making is marked by many diffeent aspects. Nevertheless, the main aspects are liability, participation, power of representation, minimum capital, and taxation.[24]

At this point, one will show, why a certain legal form was chosen.

Aspect	Shareholder A	Shareholder B
Liability	Personal liability is an option	Personal liability is not an option
Participation	Active participation is required	Provides only capital
Power of representation	Be active internally as well as externally	No liability towards management
Taxation	Income tax	Corporate tax
Compensation	Annual profit-share and salary	By contract regulated payment
Legal form	Partnership	Corporation
Outcome	Limited partnership in which a liable person is financially supported by a limited partner.	

Table No. 9: Comparison of corporation and partnership

---

[24] Wodon, Christian; Gründerservice der Wirtschaftskammer Wien (2012): p. 36 - 37

Requirements on market and competitors

Step 10: Carry out a market analysis and determine sales potentials, including sales volumes, so that lucrative sub-markets can be identified. In addition to it, one will compare the sales volume which the market can absorb with the planned sales volume the enterprise has to fulfill.

Step 11: Analyze the top five competitors in regard of the precise positioning at the market, the unique selling proposition, as well as the right adjustment of the marketing measures. At the same time an analysis of the competitive advantages or disadvantages towards the direct competitors will take place.

Step 12: With a detailed costumer analysis it is possible to create appropriate costumer segments. A clear identification of costumer segments and their needs will help the management to focus efficiently on lucrative customer segments.

6. Market and competition

In this chapter an analysis of the market where the competitors and customers meet takes place. An analysis enables one to generate information which will take an essential role by the strategical adjustment of the company.

One will finde information, as for example, profitable regions, customer segments, or relevant competitors.[25]

The information generated in this chapter can be used to strategically adjust the company in 7.2 "marketing strategy" as well as in 7.3 "marketing mix."

6.1 Market analysis

First, a market analysis refers to a branch or entire market. Step by step one enables himself to generate information which reveal the potentials of the business idea. The aim is to find out how many customers are participating at the market.

---

[25] Wodon, Christian; Gründerservice der Wirtschaftskammer Wien (2012): p. 43

To find the relevant market for the given enterprise, one can choose between different approaches. The analysis can be carried out product-, supplier-, and demand-orientated.[26]

With the product-orientated approach one defines first the service offering by the enterprise (chapter 3.2.1 „key products and services") and in the second step the possible sales regions.[27] This will help to keep track of the relevant customer segments.

Through this differentiation one will be able to estimate market potentials, market volumes, and the degree of the saturation.

Moreover, one can already predict the failure or success of the business idea by comparing the values from the sales planning with the values from the market analysis. If the values from the sales planning are higher as the values the market can absorb, then the business idea will not gain enough earnings to exist at the market in the long term.[28]

Especially important facts and figures are to be stated. The primary research method is more cost-intensive as the sec-

---

[26] Kubicek, Herbert ; Brückner, Steffen (2009): p. 117
[27] Kußmaul, Heinz (2008): p. 544
[28] Kubicek, Herbert ; Brückner, Steffen (2009): p. 118 - 119

ondary research method and only recommended if no dependable market data exist.

In the area of secondary research one will finde different sources and statistics which provide information about market and branch developments. Free sources of information are:[29]

- Chamber of Industry and Commerce
- Associations
- Federal statistical office
- Business reports of competitors
- Business register

Supply	Demand
Which offer is available at the market?	Which demand existst at the market?
How high ist he sales volume of the supply?	How high is the demand?
Who offers the service and in which region?	Which customers and regions ask generally?

Table No. 10: Requirements on a market analysis

---

[29] Wodon, Christian; Gründerservice der Wirtschaftskammer Wien (2012): p. 47

The following table will illustrate the process exemplarily which data seem relevant and to which extent. On this occasion it should be pointed out that the facts and data presented in table No. 11 are not valid.

The identified sales potentials and sales volumes are compared with the values from the budgetary planning.

Moreover, the generated information and data are used for a precise adjustment of the marketing strategy (chapter 7.2.1 „product and market strategy") and for the creation of the sales planning (chapter 9.4.1 „turnover and sales planning").

If chances and risks are to be identified from the market analysis, then these aspects are taken into account in the SWOT-Analysis.

Supply	Demand
There are four manufacturers in Germany and a total of twelve in Europe.	In Germany is only one manufacturer who produces network cards. Moreover, three manufacturers of graphic cards and six manufacturers of mainboards.
The sales of construction boards amounted last year 56 million € and 368 million € in Europe.	The sales of network cards amounted in Germany up to 3.5 million €, graphic cards 20.5 million €, and mainboards 30 million €.
The manufacturers in Europe act internationally. From twelve manufacturers in Europe ten are also distributing in Germany. There are five competitors from the USA and four from China.	Last year Germany, France, and Great Britain inquired 60 % of the existing demand for construction boards in Europe.

Table No. 11: Exemplary representation of a market analysis

6.2 Competitive analysis

Whether a business idea is crowned successfully depends not only on the market but also on the competition. A comprehensive competitive analysis encloses the direct competitors, potential new suppliers, the negotiations power of the customers, and suppliers, as well as the danger which goes out from substitutable products.[30]

Substitutable products or substitutable services are to be looked at as competitors. Butter and margarine are used during a breakfast as a spread. However, cheese spread can be used in the same manner. This means, that even if no competitive product exists, then the competitors are those companies that satisfy the current needs of the costumers.[31]

Also, potential competitors from upstream and downstream production stages will try to fill existing gaps. Therefore, companies that are currently not direct competitors should also be taken into consideration.

Basically, at the beginning the elaboration of a competitive analysis concentrates itself on the five biggest competitors and their market shares as well as on a detailed description of the main products and services.

Still, the more precise the analysis the better the strategy.

---

[30] Hauer, Georg ; Ultsch, Michael (2009): p. 20ff
[31] Wodon, Christian; Gründerservice der Wirtschaftskammer Wien (2012): p. 46

The table no. 12 „exemplary elaboration of a competitive analysis" illustrates the procedure.

competitor / criteria	Competetor 1	Competetor 2
Revenues	2 Mio. €	3 Mio. €
Market share	10 %	40 %
Price range	Los	High
Distribution channel	Sales representative and through own branches in Germany. Time to delivery: One week.	Commercial traveler and through the World Wide Web in cooperation with UPS.
Communicative appearance	Advertising statement concludes a quick and favorable solution. Advertisment is spread over the radio and regional newspapers.	Advertisement primarily on fairs and events, as for example, at the Game Com.
Key services	Mass production in the low-price sector..	Processing high-quality materials into a high-quality product.

Table No. 12: Exemplary elaboration of a competitive analysis

The generated data and information from the competitive analysis will be used to adjust the competitive strategy in chapter 7.2.2.

The identified chances and risks which arise from the analysis of the competitors are taken into account in the SWOT-Analysis.

6.3 Customer analysis[32]

Not all potential customers of the relevant market have the same interest in a certain product or service, because the needs differ from person to person or company to company. Because the needs differ, one will identify customer segments that have the same or different performance criteria.

Are customer segments identified, a precise and efficient alignment of the company as well as the marketing measures can be assured.

The first classification takes place between private and business customers. Business customers are being divided into retailers and end users.

The aim is to identify homogeneous customer segments to use their characteristics as an advantage.

---

[32] Kubicek, Herbert ; Brückner, Steffen (2009): p. 123 - 125

For example, a precise solution for a certain customer segment will generate a better customer satisfaction which allows companies to limit economic activities only on lucrative segments.

Criteria to divide private consumers into reasonable groups are, for example, age, gender, income, professional grade, life style, purchase motivation, and various behavioral characteristics, for instance, quick satisfaction or long-term investment. In general, one can distinguish between demographic, geographic, and psychographic criteria.

Presumed, one will segment private consumers by age, then it is common to divide them into appropriate groups. For example, one can combine ages between 18 years to 24 years into a group and in addition to it tie them up to distinguish characteristics that all members of the group feature.

Criteria to segment business customers or know-how orientated services one will find:

- Size of Company, supply concept
- Industry affiliation
- Technology standard,
- investment, and innovation cycles
- Order size, urgency
- Quality and certification

The compiled results from the customer analysis are not only used in chapter 7.2.1 „product and market strategy" but also in chapter 7.3 "marketing mix".

If chances and risks are identified through the elaboration of the customer analysis, then they will be taken into account in the SWOT-Analysis.

Requirements on a marketing concept

Step 13: At this point, one defines marketing goals which can be derived from the „company´s vision" or the „landmarks of the company" and determine there future state. On basis of marketing goals a strategical adjustment of the right marketing instruments takes place.

Step 14: At this Stage, one will establish one or several strategical approaches by which the defined objectives or goals are being achieved. In practice one distinguish between a product, market, as well as competitive strategy.

Step 15: At the beginning one will focus oneself on five central assignments. Identification of an (1.) unique selling proposle, the definition of (2.) a price, as well as the establishment of (3.) a distribution structure. The measurements which are taken from the communication policies during the foundation phase are limited to the areas (4.) corporate identity and (5.) advertising planning.

7. Marketing concept

Due to a holistic marketing concept, in which the overarching objectives from the company´s vision, competitive constellations, and market circumstances are being united, it is possible to adjust the instruments from the marketing mix efficiently.

By a precise and an efficient application of the instruments, one ensures maximum success.[33] In the following chapter it is described how one can develop such a marketing concept.

7.1 Marketing goals

Every concept begins with the definition of goals. The definition of qualitative and quantitative goals provide not only the possibility to reach the targeted state but also allows to control the degree of achievement.

Quantitative targets are, for example, sales figures, market share, or a certain number of customers generated per week, month, or year. On the other side, quality goals can be, for

---

[33] Stender-Monhemius, Kerstin (2002): p. 8

example, name recognition, image building, or reaching a special degree in customer satisfaction.

In the process of defining marketing goals it is enormously important to ensure, that marketing goals are not in conflict with the company´s vision. To identify possible marketing goals it makes sense to orientate oneself on chapter 3.3 „company´s vision und missions".

Note, the marketing goals must be formulated specifically and positively, so that a reaching and controlling is ensured. It means, that the goals must be „SMART": specific, measurable, acceptable, reachable, and timebound. The realization as well as the monitoring is assignable to an authority, a position, or a person.[34]

Especially companies that are in the founding phase have to ensure enough first-time customers and generate enough repeat purchases. Moreover, only long-term customer retention and steady rising sales figures can lead to success in the early stage.[35]

The following examples will illustrate the process.

---

[34] Stender-Monhemius, Kerstin (2002): p. 92
[35] Kubicek, Herbert; Brückner, Steffen (2009): p. 138

According to business plan a turnover of at least 120,000.- € have to be achieved in the first year, so that the liquidity is not endangered in the second year.

Moreover, it is evident that the planned investments can only be covered in the third year if the turnover crosses 200,000.- € in the second year.

The image, which should be associated with the company, is: reliable, top quality, and customer-friendly.

The name recognition should rise within the branch up to 75 % at the end of the fifth year.

Criterion	1. Year	2. Year	3. Year
Profi	75.000 €	100.000 €	300.000 €
Revenue	120.000 €	200.000 €	
Customer base	10	15	20
Core customers	2	4	7
Name recognition	15 %	25 %	40 %
Positive image	Quality	Service	Reliability
Customer satisfaction	80 %	85 %	90 %
Opinion leader	10.000 Follower		
Expert recognition	Award XY	20 expert articles	

Table No. 13: Exemplary representation of marketing goals

7.2 Marketing strategies

7.2.1 Product and market strategy

The product strategy and market strategy decide whether a certain service, or a certain product, or a certain customer segment stands in the focus of the business activity. The definition of the strategy encloses two considerations. On the one hand, it must be considered whether the product or service already exists in the market or not. On the other hand, whether the product or service can be imitated or innovated.

Through the fundamental determination of product and service policies as well as restricted activities on a certain customer segment the instruments from the marketing mix can be aligned conform to the company's goals.[36]

If an existing company already has different business segments, the Boston Consulting Matrix can help to find out whether it is profitable to invest in certain business divis-

---

[36] Kubicek, Herbert; Brückner, Steffen (2009): p. 139ff

ions, or to pursue an absorption, or run a disinvestment strategy.[37]

If the market growth is very high and at the same time the relative market share is very low, it is advisable to monitor the market conditions closely or to make a decision towards an investment or disinvestment strategy.

If, on the other hand, there is high market growth and at the same time a high relative market share, it is advisable to pursue an investment strategy.

If the market growth is low and the relative market share is very high, then it is advisable to pursue a disinvestment strategy.

The following exemplary representation of a Boston Consulting Matrix will illustrate the process.

---

[37] Stender-Monhemius, Kerstin (2002): p. 102

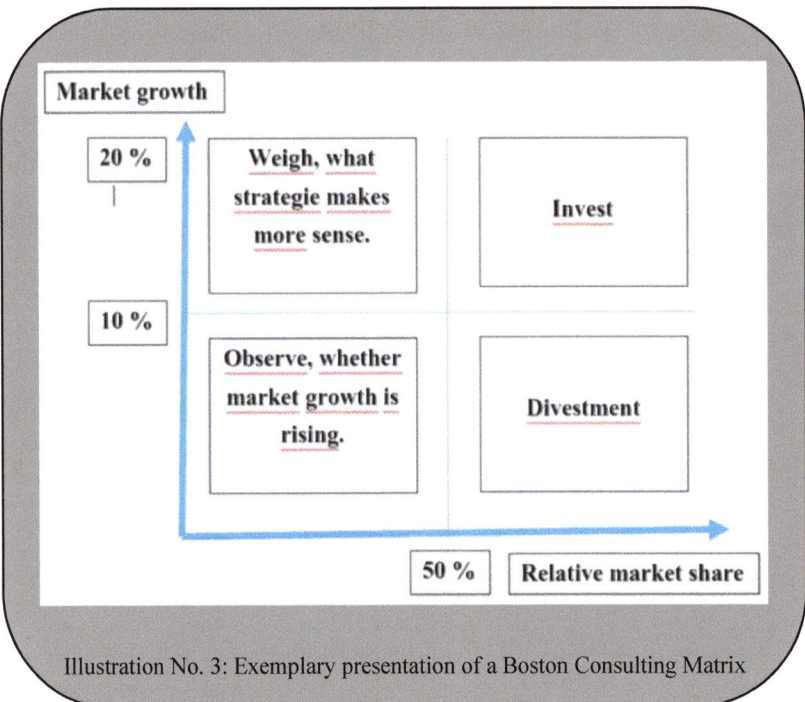

Illustration No. 3: Exemplary presentation of a Boston Consulting Matrix

The market growth for a product or service can be generated from the primary or secondary research. However, the relative market share is generated from the relation of „own market share" to „market share of the strongest competitor", or from „own turnover" to „turnover of the strongest competitor".[38]

---

[38] Reimus, Enrico: Realtiver Marktanteil

For example, the turnover of a company is 50,000.- € and the turnover of the strongest competitor is 1,000,000.- €, then the relative market share is 5 %.

The considered aspects, that are generated at this point, are being adopted in the "marketing mix" under the topic „product and performance policy" (chapter 7.3.1).

For further information to this segment the book "Marketing: Grundlagen mit Fallstudien" written by Kerstin Stender-Monhemius can be recommended.

7.2.2 Competitive strategy

To protect the success of a company, it is necessary to adopt to the market circumstances, especially to the competitors. In this regard, one has to decide whether the company will be positioned at the market as a high quality supplier or at the low price segment. Nevertheless, one has also to decide either the company will supply the entire market or specialize itself on certain customer segments.

If, for example, certain customer segments are evident which have attracted up to no or only little attention, then these customer segments have to be moved into focus. Or, one will find many competitors who lure with small prices, then it is possible to adapt to these circumstances as well.[39]

In essence, one devotes oneself either to lucrative part markets (customer segments) with little competitive pressure or one positions oneself with a clear quality advantage in the high price segment to avoid competition.

From the competitive analysis (chapter 6.2) it is already evident how the competition positioned themselves at the market. From the analysis one will be able to determine in which segment the most chances and in which segment the most risks, concerning the competitive pressure, exist.

Therefore, the generated information from the competitive analysis have to be applied at this step.

The following table will illustrate the process.

---

[39] Kubicek, Herbert ; Brückner, Steffen (2009): p. 143

Strategy / Criteria	Strategy network card	Strategy mainboard
Price range	Middle price segment	Enhanced price category
Distribution channel	Commercial traveler and through own homepage	Sales representative
Communicative appearance	Advertising statement: High-quality product for a favorable price	Advertisement at exhibitions and trade shows
Key services	Top quality product	Top quality product

Table No. 14: Exemplary representation of a competitive strategy

If difficulties or obstacles are being identified during the implementation of the strategy, then these important facts are being taken into account in the SWOT-Analysis.

Additional information to develop a competitive strategy can be find in the book "Unternehmensführung kompakt" written by Georg Hauer and Michael Ultsch.

7.3 Marketing mix

7.3.1 Product and performance policy

Product and performance policies decide what products and services are being sold or performed. Not only this but also considerations regarding the product design, product features, product package, product quality, brand policies, and services are formulated at this step.[40]

In a business plan one limits oneself by formulating the product and performance policies to the core competences. Especially in a business plan, it means to identify an unique selling proposition.

An unique selling proposition is the cornerstone of every enterprise. An unique selling proposition is used to lift, to differentiate, and to distinguish oneself from the competition.[41]

It is necessary to identify performance benefits or advantages that exist towards the customer and the competition. However, the performance benefits or advantages can also

---

[40] Kubicek, Herbert ; Brückner, Steffen (2009): p. 149
[41] Wodon, Christian; Gründerservice der Wirtschaftskammer Wien (2012): p. 24

emerge through an unique service. So, the service policies should be integrated into consideration accordingly.

In the following the process of generating an unique selling proposition will be illustrated by an example. Then, in the second step it will be shown how the service policies can be used as an advantage.

The generated costs that will occur from the product and performance policies as well as the service policies are being taken into consideration at the budgetary planning.

For more details the book „E-Entrepreneurship: Grundlagen der Unternehmensgründung in der Net Economy" written by Tobias Kollmann is recommended.

Actual situation: Construction boards at the market have a maximum tact frequency of 500 Mhz.

Wish of the customer: Construction boards with higher tact frequency and without additional power consumption.

Situation regarding the offer: Because the actual available construction boards are not able to tact higher than 500 MHz, without using additional random-access memory (RAM), the commercial use of twelve-core processors is not possible.

New offer: With the new construction boards it is possible to use twelve-core processors without additional power consumption and additional random-access memory (RAM).

Unique selling proposition: The only construction board for commercial use of twelve-core processors.

The customer is only satisfied when he receives more than he expects. So, it is necessary to think about how the service policy can offer an additional value to the customer.

Services are looked at as additional benefits. Especially at markets with a high level of competitive pressure, value-added services are the key to success.[42]

There are countless possibilities. For example, in branches with direct customer contact personality traits and the appearance of the employees are considered as very important. Because only through live interactions and conversations with the customer the personal wishes are worked out.

The company can add value and distinguish oneself from the competition by a joint and clean appearance as well as friendliness, empathy, sensitivity, and small gifts.

One can offer value-added services before the purchase, during the purchase, and also after the purchase.

---

[42] Nagl, Anna (2006): p. 48 - 50

	Service factors	Costs in €
Service bevor the purchase	Detailed consultation	
	Individual adaptation	
	Presentation or simulation	
	Quotation	
Service during the purchase	Drinks and dishes	
	Seat opportunities	
	Toilet	
	Delivery and collection service	
Service after the purchase	Warranty	
	Maintenance	
	Complaint management	
	Spare part and repair service	
	Candy	

Table No.15: Exemplary description of the service factors

7.3.2 Price policy

In this segment not only the prices of the core products or performances are set but also short-term price changes and special conditions, as for example, discounts or other price reductions.[43]

---

[43] Kubicek, Herbert ; Brückner, Steffen (2009): p. 159

The profit which decides in the final effect on success or failure arises from the difference between costs and retail price.

Besides, there are three possibilities to approach a price which is realizable at the market and at the same time yields a maximum profit. Either one orientates oneself by there own production costs (lower price limit), by the competition, or by the price the customers are willing to pay (upper price limit).[44]

In the industrial manufacturing the overhead calculation is often used to set a price or to calculate the gross profit.[45] A starting point on this occasion are the material costs and wages which can be attributed to the product or the performance directly.

On the contrary overhead expenses like storage, administrative, or canteen costs create overhead rates which are being used to spread the costs on every unit or service indirectly.[46] The sum of the direct and indirect costs is called cost price or prime cost.

---

[44] Kubicek, Herbert ; Brückner, Steffen (2009): p. 155
[45] Preißner, Andreas (2003): p. 46ff
[46] Kubicek, Herbert ; Brückner, Steffen (2009): p. 103 - 104

The retail price includes not only the costs which actually occurred but also costs like replacement value or interest rates which will occur in the future. Moreover, one has to consider that enough profit must be gained to exist at the market in the long term.

In addition, the profits are possibly used to pay the costs of living or invest in product innovations. The use of discounts, as for example, amount discounts, seasonal discounts, or cash discounts will allow one to step into contract negotiations with a certain range of action.

The calculation of the price with the help of the overhead calculation (cost + profit + discount / cash discount) enables one to set a price for every unit or service.

From branch to branch the profit margin is very different. Discounts (amount discount or seasonal discount) are usually between 5 % and 30 % and cash discounts approximately between 3 % and 5 %.[47]

Therefore, a precise formulation of the company´s terms of delivery and payment conditions is recommended.

---

[47] Jung, Hans (2006): p. 630

The following exemplary representation will illustrate the process of an overhead calculation.[48]

Direct material costs
+ Overhead material costs
= Cost of materials
Direct labour costs
+ Direct manufacturing costs
+ Overhead manufacturing costs
= Production costs
Cost of materials
+ Production costs
= Manufacturing costs
Manufacturing costs
+ Overhead administrative costs
+ Overhead distribution costs
= Total costs
Total costs
+ Profit
= Cash selling price
+ Cash discount
+ Commission
= Target retail price
+ Discount
= Retail price

[48] Glück, Oliver: Vorwärtskalkulation

7.3.3 Distribution policy

To grant the customer the access to the product or service and at the same time establish a distribution structure it is necessary to consider, how the customer can be supplied, how long does the delivery take, which sales units are most customer friendly, and all further measures that makes it easier for the customer to get in contact with the product or service. These considerations should be solved under the condition of minimizing expenses.[49]

In a business plan these questions are solved whether it will be a direct or indirect distribution channel. The distribution channel usually takes place either through commercial travelers or sales representatives, but it is also possibly to pursuit an own online trade shop or subsidiaries.

If someone decides to choose the indirect distribution channel, one has to explain whether the distribution takes place through external sales mediators, for example, wholesale, retail trade, franchise, or other authorized dealer.[50]

---

[49] Wirtz, Bernd W. (2007): p. 256
[50] Kubicek, Herbert ; Brückner, Steffen (2009): p. 161 -166

The consideration whether a direct or indirect distribution channel is an advantage depends not only on the amount of costs but also on the basis of qualitative criteria. For example, the authority to issue directives or the process of complaint handling.

The optimization of the distribution channel will be illustrated with the help of a comparison of a commercial traveler (direct distribution) and sales representative (indirect distribution).[51]

The identified costs that arise from the distribution policies are being considered in the budgetary planning. The considerations which arise from the distribution structure are also used in chapter 5 „management and organization".

For further information the book "Marketing: Lehr- und Handbuch" written by Werner Pepels can be recommended.

---

[51] Pepels, Werner (2001): p. 80ff

Criterion	Travelling salesman	Sales representetive
Legal basis	Employment contract	Agency contract
Legal positon	Employee with attorney	Independent trader
Occupation	In the name and on calculation of the employer	In foreign name on foraign calculation
Sales channel	Direct	Indirect
Rights	Equal rights as employees	Right on information, documents, samples and commission
Obligations	Effort, notification, as well as loyalty duty, and duty of confidentiality	Effort, notification, diligence, discretion, travel reports, and no distribution of competitive products
Compensation	Fixed amount + commission	Commission

Table No. 16: Comparison between commercial traveler and sales representative

7.3.4 Communication policy

In this chapter, it is time to describe how one will create attention for himself or the company and which information will be shared to persuade the customer of the product or service. Furthermore, it is important to describe how one will stay in contact with the customer in the long term.

Besides, the goal at this step is not only to inform and convince business related groups but also to create a dialogue. In this regard there are various instruments and measurements that will create the desired effect.[52]

In the early stage it is common to limit oneself to a holistic corporate identity and a holistic advertising planning.

A corporate identity describes the uniform appearance of the company towards the customer[53] and consists of the following areas:[54]

- Corporate Culture (company´s philosophy)
- Corporate Design (appearance of the company)
- Corporate Behavior (uniform code of conduct)
- Corporate Communication (coordinated communication)

The goal is to generate a positive image and a strong identity. If the employees or customers identify themselves with the generated image, then it can increase the satisfaction of

---

[52] Kubicek, Herbert ; Brückner, Steffen (2009): p. 55
[53] Birkigt, Klaus ; Stadler, Marinus M.; Funck, Hans Joachim (2002): p. 161
[54] Rode, Verena (2004): p. 66

the employees and customers. In this manner a holistic corporate identity can contribute to the company´s success.[55]

In the early stage of business activities it is recommended
to increase fame, generate many new customers, persuade
customers of the product, service, and overall performance,
as well as to reach a high customer loyalty.

Because advertisement is used to inform, convince, and to
animate customers to take action, it is also recommended to
create a holistic advertising planning.

The costs of the communication policies are taken into consideration at the budgetary planning under the topic "marketing".

The planning, realization, and controlling of an advertising
planning can be divided in six phases.[56]

    1. Goal of the advertisement

    2. Choice of the target group or region

    3. Set advertising budget

    4. Choice of the advertising material and design

---

[55] Regenthal, Gerhard (2009): p. 17
[56] Nagl, Anna (2006): p. 55

5. Realization of the campaign

6. Control of the advertising measurements

As a result, one will receive a list of the advertising measures including the total costs.

The following table will illustrate the process.

Advertising goal	Inform and convince the customers	Inform customers
Advertising object	Product or service X	Company
		Performance range
Media	Magazine X	Website
Materials	Text	Video
	Graphic	Text
	Company´s logo	Company´s logo
Advertisers	Individual advertising	Mass advertising
Advertising period	03.01. - 16.01.2020	All year round for the duration of 2 to 4 years
	10.10. - 12.12.2020	
Total cost	1. Advertising period 495.- €	279.- € per year
	2. Advertising period 995.- €	Production costs approx. 985.- €

Table No. 17: Exemplary representation of an advertising planning

Requirements on a SWOT-Analysis

Step 16: Identification of strengths and weaknesses which surround the company. For example, competences, finances, and all other performance advantages or disadvantages which come to light during the process of editing the single steps and chapters.

Step 17: At this step, it is necessary to filter out the chances and risks which arise immediately from the environment. One will consider areas, as for example, competitors, customers, suppliers, research facilities, and political influences.

Step 18: To conclude the SWOT-Analysis a confrontation between company´s strengths or weaknesses and environmental´s chances and risks will take place at this point. Out of such a confrontation one can develop strategies for relevant circumstances. In addition to the development of strategies one will try to predict how the rising obstacles will effect the company and of course how likely a certain scenario will occure in the future.

8. SWOT-Analysis

The business plan is a snapshot, however, it is to be noted that the company as well as the environment are permanently confronted with changes. So, it makes sense to think about future events.

Therefor, one looks at the company´s internal strengths and weaknesses to confront them with the chances and risks which arise immediately from the environment. With this step, strengths can be used to exploit chances or to neutralise or minimise risks.

Entrepreneurial strengths are, for example, special skills, advanced industry knowledge of the people involved, a high equity ratio, or a product innovation. The identification of strengths and weaknesses results on the one hand from the requirements considered above and on the other hand from the monetary perspective revealed through the financial planning.

Opportunities that arise from the environment are, for example, a lack of competitors, government subsidies, or changes in customer preferences. If there are no opportunities to be identified from the environment, then it does not automatically represent risks, but current conditions that should be used as an advantage as much as possible.

One distinguishes four strategies: Exploit, searching, confrontation, or avoid.

If, for example, you have identified opportunities that arise from the environment during the analysis phase, one can try to exploit them through own entrepreneurial strengths.

If, on the other hand, favorable environmental factors meet entrepreneurial weaknesses, then one should find ways to convert weaknesses into strengths in order to take advantage of the environmental conditions.

If external influencing factors represent risks, then it is advisable to use entrepreneurial strengths to minimize or mitigate them.

If there are no entrepreneurial strengths, it is advisable to avoid external risks.

The following SWOT-Matrix will illustrate the process.

SWOT-Analysis and strategy		Analysis of the internal resources and abilities	
		Strengths	Weeknesses
Analysis of the external factors of influence	Chances	**Exploit** - Which strengths can be used to use the existing chances successfully and optimally?	**Searching** - Which weaknesses allow to take chances or must be overcome to be able to perceive chances?
	Risks	**Confrontation** - Which strengths can be used to minimize or neutralize risks?	**Avoid** – On behalf of the constellation between risks and weaknesses, what serious threats can be identified?

Table No. 18: SWOT-Analysis

The forecast of future events is not always easy. Neverthe-less, one is able to identify single environmental states and trends as well as strength and weaknesses of the business idea or company. With the help of the scenario technique one is able to simplify certain scenarios. In addition, identified key factors are also valued in the probability of occurrence.

The normal-case-scenario stands for the option with the highest probability to occur. In any case, one will value every key factor on how a worst-case-scenario, a normal-case-scenario, and a best-case-scenario will impact the business idea or enterprise.

The assessment of positive scenarios can be expressed by positive signs (+, or ++) and negative developments can be expressed with negative signs (-, or - -).[57] The following table will illustrate the process.

Key factor	Scenarios	Effect
Technology	Best-Case	+ +
	Normal-Case	+
	Worst-Case	-
Market growth	Best-Case	+ +
	Normal-Case	+ +
	Worst-Case	+
Liquidity	Best-Case	+
	Normal-Case	- -
	Worst-Case	- -

Table No. 19: Assessment of the probability of possible scenarios and their effects on the company

---

[57] Kubicek, Herbert ; Brückner, Steffen (2009): p. 193 - 199

The analysis of the external environmental factors partially occurred in the chapter 6 „market and competitors" as well as chapter 7.2 "marketing strategy" and should be taken into consideration at this point.

The analysis of the internal abilities and resources occurred in chapters "company presentation", „factory and operating equipment", as well as „management and organization".

Requirements on financial planning and executive summary

Step 19: Exposure of the exact capital requirements and description of the protection of sufficient funds in a period between three to five years.

Step 20: In step 20 the calculation and planning of the profit or loss in a period between three to five years takes place.

Step 21: At this point, one provides a liquidity planning. It means that one calculates and plans the actual deposits and payments.

Step 22: Complementary calculations to fulfill the needs of a meaningful budgetary planning are, for example, sales planning, production planning, supply planning, personnel planning, and investment planning.[58]

Step 23: As a final step a summary of the most important information which has been generated from these areas are mentioned. The summary in a business plan is called „executive summary".

---

[58] Nagl, Anna (2006): p. 72 – 75

9. Finance planning

The finance planning checks the business idea concerning the economic efficiency and therefore the feasibility for a period between three to five years.

To do so, turnover and yields are compared with the costs and expenses, so that the generated profit or loss will be clearly evident in the profit planning.

The core of the finance planning consists of the capital requirements planning, finance planning, profit and loss calculation, as well as the liquidity planning.

Complementary plans, for example, sales, production, procurement, personnel, investment, or write-off planning are essential and builds the base of the finance planning.[59]

In chapter 9.4 „complementary planning" the most important ones will be introduced.

---

[59] Nagl, Anna (2006): p. 17 - 18

9.1 Capital requirements and finance planning

In this segment, it is necessary to filter out how much capital is needed to realize the business idea and on the other hand to indicate which sources of financing can be used and to what extent the financing must be accessible.

For medium-sized and big capital companies the legislator gives with the §§ 266 II, III from the commercial code an arrangement on how to structure capital requirements and financial plans.

The layout orientate itself on an opening balance sheet. On the assets page (on the left) one will record everything what is required to start the commercial activity.

After everything was written down that is necessary to start the business activity, one describes on the liabilities page (on the right) the capital requirements and how they are financed. The sum of the liabilities must correspond to the sum of the assets.[60]

The following table (No. 20) will illustrate the process.

---

[60] Nagl, Anna (2006): p. 80

1. Tangible assets	€	1. Equity	€
Property and buildings		Cash	
Factory equipment		Material assets	
Market research		Venture capital	
…		…	
Total investments	35,000	Total equity	40,000
2. Operating material		**2. Public funds**	
Goods and materials		Micro-credit	
Raw, auxiliary, and operating materials		Start-up fund	
Prefinancing orders		KfW entrepreneuer credit	
Company car		Equity support	
…		…	
Gesamte Betriebsmittel	13,000	Gesamte öffentliche Mittel	8,000
3. Start-up costs		**3. Credits**	
Tax and legal consultancy		Credit 1	
Handouts / travaling / professional development		Credit 2	
Opening costs		Privat investor	
Franchise fee		Strategic investor	
Commission / deposit		Business Angel	
…		…	
Total start-up costs	2,000	Total credit	2,000
Whole amount to be financed	**50,000**	**Whole amount of funds**	**50,000**

Table No. 20: Exemplary representation of an opening balance sheet

9.2 Profit and loss calculation

In the profit and loss calculation (revenue planning) one calculates the planned operating result and the result after taxes. The exact planned profit or loss of the company. The calculation can occur either on the basis of the total cost method or the cost of sales method.

During the total cost method all taxable turnover will be subtracted by the operating expenditures. The costs which are not of operational nature can lead afterwards to additional tax payments. Of course, costs that set too high or too low falsify the operating result and the economic efficiency of the company what leads to the fact that the significance of the business plan will be affected.

Afterwards, one subtracts from the generated operational turnover the direct and indirect expenditures (total costs) in order to calculate the result before tax deduction. If it is, for example, a production-based company in which the product is made from several components it is recommended to tangle a production plan, so that the direct costs can be identified exactly.

The running and indirect expenditures can be taken from the written part in particular form the chapters „factory and operating equipment", „management and organization", as well as "marketing mix".

At last, it is to be checked whether one is amenable to the income tax, corporation tax, or even both.

Which legal form was chosen can be taken from chapter 5.3 „legal form".

The business taxes which are raised by the resident community are subjected to very strong differences and need to be discovered from city to city.

The following table (No. 21) corresponds to the basic pattern of the § 275 II commercial code.[61]

---

[61] Nagl, Anna (2006): p. 76

1. Year / 2. Year / 3. Year	January	February	March
Turnover			
- Referring achievements and goods (direct expenditures)			
Gross profit			
- Indirect expenses			
Management salaries			
Personnel			
Room costs			
Office costs			
Energy costs			
Low-value assets			
Vehicle costs			
Marketing and sales			
Business insurance			
Tax and legal consultancy			
Travel expenses			
Depreciation			
Intrest			
Other expenses			
Total expenses			
Earnings bevor taxes			
Income tax			
Corporate tax			
Business tax			
Earnings after tax deduction			

Table No. 21: Exemplary representation of a profit and loss calculation

9.3 Liquidity planning

At first sight the liquidity plan looks like the revenue plan. However, the profit and loss calculation are about turnovers and expenditures, whereas the liquidity plan examines the actual and exact deposits and payments.

Between the operating turnovers and the payments mostly lies a temporal delay. Costs arise as soon as one produces a product or a service. However, the payment (operating turnovers) occurs when the customer actually pays.

According to branches it can last several weeks or even months until the product or the service will be paid by the customer. This discrepancy between deposits and payments should be considered in the installation of the liquidity plan. So, whether future invoices can be paid or not.

This is very important because lacking liquidity can automatically lead to bankruptcy. If the running payment is greater than the running deposits, what is mostly the case at the beginning, then the gaps will be closed by own funds, loan, credit, or with an overdraft.[62]

---

[62] Nagl, Anna (2006): p. 82

1. Year / 2. Year / 3. Year	January	February	March
Turnover			
Value added tax			
Sum of running deposits			
Referring achievements and goods			
Personal drawing			
Sum of running payments			
Liquidity balance of running payments			
Tangible assets			
Operating material			
Togal payments for investments			
Public funds			
Credit			
Total payments for investments			
Liquidity balance of payments for investments			
Total balance of liquidity			
Cumulative liquidity			

Table No. 22: Exemplary representation of a liquidity planning

9.4 Complementary planning

9.4.1 Turnover and sales planning

The sales planning is the most important component of a business plan, because only the amount of the sold products or services allows a realistic approve of the commercial activity for a long period of time.[63]

Therefore, it is necessary to provide a realistic sales plan for a period between three to five years.

Of course, one can never know how much sales will be generated. Rather, one will have to give realistic numbers which orientate themselves on the analysis of the customer target group, market circumstances, and competitors.

On the other side, the sales figures will not be left completely to coincidence, but can be steered through different marketing activities.

In most cases the sales figures are low in the first six months and then rise slowly. Moreover, is to be considered that many branches are subject to seasonal fluctuations.[64] Chap-

---

[63] Nagl, Anna (2006): p. 72 - 73
[64] Klandt, Heinz ; Finke-Schürmann, Tanja (2000): p. 98 - 99

ter 6 „market and competitors" offers good approaches to do analysis and forecasts.

The considerations which were carried out in chapter „market analysis" should also flow into the sales planning. The compiled results from the turnover and sales planning will be adopted in chapter 9.3 "liquidity planning".

In the early stages one limits himself to five sales units or services, because a comprehensive forecast confuses rather than clarify.

One takes five products or services (chapter 3.2.1 „key products and services"), and sets how many (indication of quantity) can be sold through a standard month for a period between three to five years.

The table No. 23 will illustrate the approach.

Product, or service	1. Year Quantity per month	2. Year Quantity per month	3. Year Quantity per month	Total turnover
Turnover unit 1	500	700	1,500	32,400
Turnover unit 2				
Turnover unit 3				
Turnover unit 4				
Turnover unit 5				

Table No. 23: Exemplary presentation of a sales and turnover planning

If the forecast of the sales figures in the first three years are as realistic as possible, then in the second step the assessment of the seasonal fluctuations takes place.[65]

There are strong months and there are weak months, so, one should not only know the customary high-level and low-level points but also take it into consideration. For example, a hotel has other peak times than a vehicle repair shop.

---

[65] Neuhäuser, Rainer (2001): p. 52

The judgement of high-level or low-level months will be made on the basis of positive and negative sign. One positive sign „+" for a strong sales month and two positive signs „+ +" for a very strong sales month.

As a countermove, weak months for sales are marked with a negative sign „-", and very weak months with two negative signs „- -". However, a usual standard month is marked with a zero „0".

1. Year	J	F	M	A	M	J	J	A	S	O	N	D
TU 1	-	+	++	+	0	--	-	-	0	+	+	-
TU 2												
TU 3												
TU 4												
TU 5												

Table No. 24: Assessment of seasonal fluctuations

9.4.2 Investment and depreciation planning

Tangible and intangible assets which value of acquisitions was more than 800.- € (net) and will be used several years may not be written-off directly as a whole expenditure in the revenue planning but through the duration of use.

The write-off planning complements therefore the liquidity planning. In fact, the acquisition value or production cost will be spread over the ordinary useful life and taken into account as a depreciation in the liquidity planning.

That means, that tangible and intangible assets are losing a part of their production cost or acquisition value very year.[66]

To determine the total amount of the annual write-off sum, one list all assets to a write-off plan.

The ordinary useful life of an economic good is evident from the table „deduction of wear and tear" and is published by the Federal Ministry of Finances.

---

[66] Kubicek, Herbert ; Brückner, Steffen (2009): p. 232 - 233

It is to be noted, this step concerns economic and not tax aspects.

	Write-offs 1. Year / 2. Year / 3. Year		
	Acquisition value	Useful life	Amount of write-offs
Production			
Unit	10,000 €	10 Years	1,000 €
R & D			
Measure instrument	5,000 €	15 Jahre	333.33 €
Distribution			
Company car	9,000 €	4 Jahre	2,250 €
Administration			

Table No. 25: Exemplary presentation of a write-off planning

The economic goods for the write-off planning are found in chapter 4 "factory and operating equipment" as well as Chapter 9.1 „capital requirements and finance planning".

Afterwards, the calculated depreciations will be taken into account in the profit and loss calculation as well as liquidity planning.

9.4.3 Personnel planning

The personnel planning consists of two components. The number of the employees and the total cost. The personnel planning indicates how high the costs are and in which functional areas they accrue. It serves, like every sub plan, the traceability and builds the basis of the finance planning.[67]

The personnel plan can be reconstructed from the chapter 5 „management and organization". The costs of the employees will be invoiced proportionally.

A salary comparison sorted by occupational groups and regions can be find regularly on the World Wide Web, for example, at www.netto-lohn.de.

The following approach will illustrate an exemplary presentation of a personnel planning.

---

[67] Nagl, Anna (2006): p. 75

	Personnel 1. Year		Personnel 2. Year	
	Amount	in T €	Amount	in T €
Production	2	50	5	250
R & D				
Sales				
Distribution				

Table No. 26: Exemplary presentation of a personnel planning

9.4.4 Privat demand

In this segment, one determines the amount of private demand represented in money. This amount flows into the finance planning and will give a reference point to see whether one can live from the profits which the company generates in the long term.

For self-employed ones the private demand is higher than for regular employees, because the self-employed ones have to pay their insurances from private funds.

It is to be noted, payments have to be taken into account in the month in which they occur. For example, in the beginning of the year the car insurance will be paid. In summer the holiday payment and in December the Christmas bonus.

A monthly amount of 100.- € through the whole year for the additional payments will not fulfill the needs of a realistic liquidity plan.[68]

It does very little, if one wants to save the money in the course of the year, but the liquidity, because of other payments, does not allow it. It comes to payment bottlenecks what can lead to disagreeable negotiations with the capital providers, for example, the house bank.

1. Year / 2. Year / 3. Year			
Privat expenses	January	February	March
Rent and additional costs			
Food			
Insurance			
Cloth			
Vacation			
Contributions for leisure activities and associations			
Car			
Other expenses			
Total amount of expenses			
Privat income			
Child benefit			
Interim payment			
Incomes of husband			
Other income			
Total income			
Privat need			

Table No. 27: Examplary calculation of a private demand

[68] Wodon, Christian; Gründerservice der Wirtschaftskammer Wien (2012): p. 64 - 65

10. Executive summary

A business plan always begins with a summarized descript-tion of the business idea. An executive summary is there-fore a short presentation of the business model or business plan and should wake up different claim groups, for exam-ple, customers, banks, advisers, Chambers of Industry and Commerce, or shareholders who have a mutual interest at the business idea and the business plan itself.

An executive summary has a length of maximum two to three pages and introduces briefly, exactly, and understand-ably all-important data and statements.

Mostly, the executive summary is written after the prepara-tion of the business plan, because many questions deserve an exact analysis and elaboration.

In addition, a business model can be shown graphically in an executive summary. This will make the idea or concept clearer and more accessible.

The following questions should be discussed in an execu-tive summary.[69]

---

[69] Nagl, Anna (2006): p. 19

- What is the business idea and which products or services are offered?
- What is the unique selling proposition and which use will everyone have?
- Who is the customer target group?
- How does the offer reach the target group?
- How big is the market potential and which trends can be predicted?
- Which competitive advantages can be set up?
- What are the short-, medium-, and long-term goals of the company?
- Which qualifications are owned by the founder's team or the management?
- Which landmarks are the most important to convert the plan?
- Which risks and chances are worth mentioning?
- How high are the capital requirements?
- What are the expectations of yields and profits?

A table of content which makes it easier to orientated one-self through the document will follow the executive summary.[70]

The main arrangement points are:

- Company presentation

- Factory and operating equipment

- Management und organization

- Market und competitors

- Marketing

- SWOT-Analysis

- Finance planning

[70] Kubicek, Herbert ; Brückner, Steffen (2009): p. 67 - 71

11. Summary

The editing process of a business plan according to defined leading questions reveals that the requirements for a holistic business concept can be described in 23 steps.

Nevertheless, the amount of work differs very strong from step to step. It is due to the fact that the single steps are connected like building blocks which will result in one great building at the end.

On the other hand, the editing process of the single steps is bound to the enterprise and their environmental influences. This leads to different focuses and accuracies in the elaboration.

The 23 steps only show basic considerations and every step can be deepened and extended accordingly to the business idea.

In steps 1 to 12 an analysis and prediction of the business idea and the structure of the enterprise occurs as a whole. Through the eleboration one will find the arrangements of the enterprise which consists of the company´s presentation, description of the factory and operating equipment, the production range, as well as services.

The arrangements referring the management and organization are included. At last, a detailed description of the market circumstances, competitors, and customer target groups follows.

As a result of the elaboration of the minimum requirements information will be set free which are essential to successfully transform the business idea into a long-term company.

Furthermore, the generated information will also be used to create a holistic marketing concept and detailed SWOT-Analysis as well as within a detailed finance planning.

In the steps 13 to 15 the enterprise´s activities are divided into operational and strategical measures. A specific alignment as well as an efficient application of the measures enables one to realize the business plan.

Through the steps 16 to 18 an evaluation of the whole business plan occurs, while one confronts the strengths and weaknesses of the enterprise with the chances and risks that appear through the environment. A forecast of prospects and a cooresponding strategy will be generated to use the available chances, hurdles, and barriers properly.

Through the steps 19 to 22 one grasps all information which arise from the compiled steps and creates an economic approach of the business idea. The minimum requirements on a finance planning deliver as a result a short table of capital requirements and liabilities, a profit and loss calculation, as well as a liquidity planning for a period between three to five years.

As an important step, if this does not occur already elsewhere, one provides subpart plans which are essential for the calculation of the enterprise`s success. At this stage, one will find turnover planning, investment planning, write-off plans, personnel planning, and also calculations of the private demand.

If one has compiled all 22 steps, then one provides at the last step a summary (executive summary) of all-important data regarding the business idea and uses it as an introduction. The arrangement of an executive summary is short and precise, so that a mutual interest in the following document occur.

Business Plan

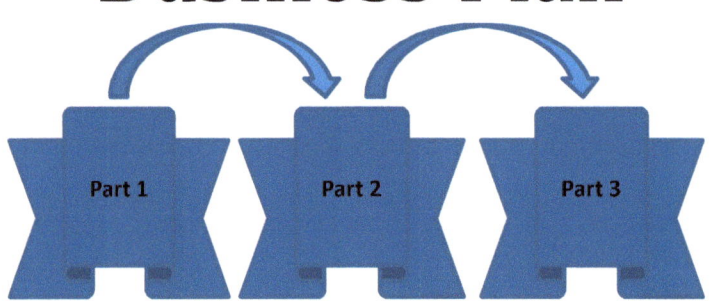

Part 1   Part 2   Part 3

Detailed description
of the chances of
success…

…in 23 steps.

12. Bibliography

Birkigt, Klaus; Stadler, Marinus M.; Funck, Hans Joachim (2002): Corporate Identity. 11. überarbeitete und aktualisierte Auflage.. München: MI Wirtschaftsbuch, (2002).

Camphausen, Bernd (2008): Grundlagen der Betriebs-wirts-wirtschaftslehre: Bachelor Kompaktwissen. München: Oldenbourg Verlag, 2008.

Glück, Oliver: Vorwärtskalkulation in: http://www.welt-der-bwl.de/Vorw%C3%A4rtskalkulation (Stand: 02.11.16)

Hauer, Georg; Ultsch, Michael (2009): Unternehmens-führung kompakt. München: Oldenbourg Verlag, 2009.

Jung, Hans (2006): Allgemeine Betriebswirtschaftslehre. Überarbeitete Auflage. München: Oldenbourg Verlag, 2006.

Karbach, Rolf; Niederle, Jan (2004): Grundlagen der Unternehmensführung: eine kompakte Darstellung für den schnellen Einstieg. Altenberge: Niederle-Media, 2004.

Klandt, Heinz; Finke-Schürmann, Tanja (2000): Existenzgründung für Hochschulabsolventen. So erstellen Sie

einen überzeugenden Business Plan. Überarb. Aufl.
Frankfurt am Main: Eichborn Verlag Ag, 2000.

Kollmann, Tobias (2009): E-Entrepreneurship: Grundlagen der Unternehmensgründung in der Net Economy. 3.
überarb. u. erw. Aufl. 2009. GWV Fachverlag GmbH,
Wiesbaden, 2009.

Kubicek, Herbert; Brückner, Steffen (2009): Business-
pläne für IT-basierte Geschäftsideen: Betriebswirtschaft-
liche Grundlagen anhand von Fallstudien. 1. Aufl. Heidel-
berg: Dpunkt.Verlag GmbH, 2009.

Kußmaul, Heinz (2008): Betriebswirtschaftslehre für Ex-
istenzgründer: Grundlagen mit Fallbeispielen und Fragen
der Existenzgründungspraxis. 6. vollst. überarb. u. erw. A.
München: Oldenbourg Verlag, 2008.

Lausen, Uwe H. (2010): Kalte Fusion Bestätigt. Globalkey
– eine Privatinitiative zum Erhalt der Arbeit des ehemaligen
live Net Concept 2010 e.V. In URL:
http://www.globalkey.de/technik/kalte-fusion-
bestaetigt.html, 02.05.2013.

Nagl, Anna (2006): Der Businessplan – Geschäftspläne professionell erstellen: Mit Checklisten und Fallbeispielen. 3. überarb. und erw. Aufl. 2006. Berlin: Springer DE, 2006.

Neuhäuser, Rainer (2001): Schnellkurs: Betriebswirtschaft für start-ups: mit kühlem Kopf durch den Finanz- und Kostendschungel. Regensburg: Walhalla Fachverlag, 2001.

Pepels, Werner (2001): Einführung in das Distributionsmanagement. Völlig überarbeitete Auflage. München: Oldenbourg Verlag, 2001.

Pepels, Werner (2004): Marketing: Lehr- und Handbuch. Völlig überarbeitete und erweiterte Auflage. München: Oldenbourg Verlag, 2004.

Preißner, Andreas (2003): Kalkulation und Preispolitik. 1. Aufl.. München, Wien: Hanser Verlag, 2003.

Reimus, Enrico: Relativer Marktanteil in: http://www.controllingportal.de/Fachinfo/Grundlagen/Kennzahlen/relativer-Marktanteil.html (Stand: 02.11.2016).

Regenthal, Gerhard (2009): Ganzheitliche Corporate Identity: Profilierung von Identität und Image. Berlin: Springer DE, 2009.

Rode, Verena (2004): Corporate Branding von Gründungsunternehmen: Der Erfolgreiche Aufbau der Unternehmensmarke. Berlin: Springer DE, 2004.

Sabisch, Helmut (1999): Management technologieorientierter Unternehmensgründungen. Helmut Sabisch (Hrsg.). Schäffer-Poeschel Verlag, Stuttgart, 1999.

Sadowski, Ulf; Gläß, Michaela (2010): Der Business Plan als kritischer Pfad strategischen Managements. In: Was heisst und zu welchem Ende studiert man ... Management? 1. Aufl. Plauen: M-&-S-Verlag, 2010, S. 145 – 162.

Stender-Monhemius, Kerstin (2002): Marketing: Grundlagen mit Fallstudien. München: Oldenbourg Verlag, 2002.

Wien, Andreas (2009): Existenzgründung. München: Oldenbourg Wissensch.Vlg, 2009.

Wirtz, Bernd W. (2007): Multi-Channel-Marketing: Grundlagen - Instrumente - Prozesse. Berlin: Springer DE, 2007.

Wodon, Christian; Gründerservice der Wirtschafts-kammer Wien (2012): Keine Angst vor dem Business Plan – Ein Handbuch für Gründerinnen und Gründer. 4. Auflage, Wien 2012. I2b – ideas to business, Initiative zur Erstellung eines Unternehmenskonzeptes. In URL: http://www.i2b.at/content.aspx?sm=1&men=45&AID=95, 29.03.2013.

13. List of tables

14. List of figures